Lithium Dreams And Melancholy Sunrise

Lithium Dreams And Melancholy Sunrise

By: Carrie Lowrance

To my friends and family for always supporting me.

To those that inspired this poetry, you know who you are.

Contents

Lithium Dreams And Melancholy Sunrise

Note

I feel the fire of rage burning within me
The invisible pain fills my heart
Blue blood trickling from a heart barely beating
The full moon drives me to insanity
As I sit alone in painful peace
Waiting for you to come back, you see

Through my tear filled eyes I see
The constant sadness that dwells inside me
Lost in a world of darkened peace
My seemingly un-beating heart
Leads me to insanity
Because of its un-beating

Always un-beating
Memories flashing in your mind, you see
Are they driving you to insanity?
Like the memories in my mind are doing to me?
My broken heart
Struggling for painless peace

Painless peace
A restoration of constant beating
Starting at the bottom of my heart
So I'm new again, you see
A yearning to go on burns in me
But I can't because of empty insanity

Empty insanity
Painful peace
Struggling inside me
Heart helplessly beating
How I long for you to look and see
The pain in my heart

The pain in my heart
My mind filled with insanity
Everyday I look and see
My emotions fighting my mind for peace
Swirling, beating
To be released from me
The heart un-beating, the mind filled with insanity
The memories that haunt me and pain you'll never see
My heart fighting to start beating

Darkness

Gray skies
Gray skies
So dark and yet so bright
'Causing me to shield my eyes

Squinting, squinting in the light of day
When the comfort of darkness is so suddenly taken away
Forced into the light
Forced away from my solitude
Where my thoughts roam and emotions brew
Going out into the dim light
Taming my restless soul
Longing for darkness
Where I finally feel whole

Retreating to my coffin
My deep, black hole
Where I can't be seen
Content is my soul
Safe and alone
These four walls, like a prison, are my home
Where my mind is free and emotions roam

In a few hours time
Light rears its ugly head
Once again my soul is dead
Faded into a world
Wondering amongst them
Yearning for darkness to set
When I can live again

Lobotomy

Feeling the cutting
The sawing through my skull
Pain shoots through me
Though to me it feels like a massage

Feeling the instruments
Stirring so easily
Liquid oozing
Thoughts being freed
Removing a part of me

My skull falls back into place
Perfect fit, not covering my face
Gauze surrounding me
Wrapped tightly to keep things in place
So no brain runs down my face
They tell me now I'll be perfectly fine
In a few days time
That I'm no longer crazy

Blackness

Blackness
Blackness overcoming me
Covering my feet, face and body
Filling my mind with peace
Strangers there to protect me
Drifting, drifting to sub consciousness
Drowning in the deep abyss
Blackness, blackness swallow me whole
Sinking into the soft, mink stole
Arms around me
My mind is free
Slowly, slowly the clock ticks by
Till the sky starts to fry
The vultures lie in wait
To get me and take me away
Next sweet day

Anchored

A hand grabs a hold of me
I wish it would let go
But it won't let me be
Stop! Stop!
You're anchoring my soul
It's disturbing me
I feel it panic in silent desperation
So afraid it will never move again
Finally, finally you set me free
And I can move again
My soul moving with me
Once again free

Faded

The day has dawned cold
Bone-chilling dark and cold
I walk around, a living shadow
Cloaked in emotions darkened glow
I look in the mirror
Into my eyes
There is no life there
The lips a thin line
Never smiling
Feel like I've been sleeping for years
My heart says one thing but my body won't let go
Feeling so old as the day is young
Lacking energy
My emotions a swirling mist inside
Day by day
They slowly fade
Deeper, deeper inside of me
My soul cries out, a silent plea
Feeling so invisible
Though life is livable
I am not miserable
For forever I'll be
Feeling faded

Disappear

Longing, longing
To be in the ground six foot deep
Air circling above me, not covered over
Animals and vultures watch me as I sleep
Shadows nearby to protect me
So none of the others can get me
Sleeping, sleeping so peacefully
Where they can't find me
Until the sunlight blinds me

Void

Sitting in my prison
Slight stirring of insanity inside me
Feeling a little paranoid
The vultures mistook the cord for a worm
Causing my void
My communication ceasing
Longing to speak
To speak to those
Those of who I was forced to flee
Now drowning in my need
To fill the void

Obsession

Silently, silently stalking you
Down every city street and country road you choose
Blackness my companion, night vision is my guide
Watching, watching, biding my time
I will never leave
My ears hear every breath you breathe
Every sigh you heave
Every pounding heartbeat
Every tear you cry
Falling from your face, the sky
Every word you sing
I watch every game you play
In your beautiful life during night and day
I watch you sleep during the night
As you cry out in your sleep
For the vampire bite
As you cry out for me
For the one who'll make you free
As the blood seeps
Flowing, flowing into me

You are now mine
Into solitude I'll flee
Bound together forever
We will be

Missing You (Tears)

Blood, blood falling from the sky
As rivers of blue blood fall from my eyes
The ache that's felt from my heart to my ankles and wrists
My nights of sleep deprivation
From insomnia tic fits
The heaviness of my eyes
In broad daylight
My mind unable to function
From being up part of the night
Saline and emotion trickling from me
Crying heart dripping blood beads
Dying for you to come home
And set me free
From worry

Eyes

Eyes, eyes
Rolling back into my head
To look at my innards
And see my soul is dead

Funeral

At the crossroads I am standing
Am I in heaven or am I in hell
Surrounded by those, those who knew you so well
Now you're sleeping peaceful
I close my eyes and pray
That you'll be strong tomorrow
And heaven's light will shine upon your face
Though I know your life didn't point you that way
God and I are bargaining
Off in the distance I hear voices
Talking to you, talking to me
Sympathies wasted on our hollow shells
As I grieve for alone for you, in my private hell
I sink to the ground, bleeding soul
Deserted in my heart
Hoping and praying I'll see you again
Deceiving myself in that
I never will

Standing by desire's pool

Standing by desire's pool
My body and soul bare
Yet steaming
Feelings seeping
Curling up in wisps from my veins
Staring at the horizon
Through the haze
I see your penetrating gaze
Prolonging the fires at bay
Burning in my heart, burning in your eyes
Wanting to set the world on fire
With this desire
To drink the water from the sea
Drunk on love eternally

Deserted

Wandering, wandering
Down twisted roads and dark alleys
The night so black it's blue
Looking for someone-looking for you
A stray cat my companion
I know you're hiding
Hiding from me
The reason why, I can't see
Gone
Gone for days, weeks, months
Each passing second my heart grows weak
In the panic and desperation
I search
Knowing you're lost in your life
In friendship I've grown to love you
Though your commitment to most would offend
Deceiving those who think you'll be around to the end
My soul does die
My body bends

A cold, cold wind blows through me
No soul, no soul
I lie on the swollen ground
Flooded by rain and tears
Deserted in my heart

Elation Accident

Death descends upon me
My soul writhes in ecstasy
As its voice cries out in terror
At the shower of splintered glass all around
An arctic air blows through my soul
Pain shoots through me, keeping my body warm
I turn my head slowly to the side
My head feeling decapitated
From my body and skin, my hide
I see you lying there
Your body bent and torn
Subconsciously I start to mourn
My eyes start to bleed
Mixing with crimson rivers flowing from me
The heavy cologne of your addiction
Intoxicates me
I feel myself slipping
Desperately, weakly, I make one last plea
Please, please bury him with me
Hoping someone will hear me

My spirit takes flight, still in earthly agony
As I drift toward the light
I look back and see
The demons descending upon thee
Now I look down and see
The tomb in which lies him and me
Lying peaceful by the sea

Bleeding

Lying here in silence
As emotional death comes upon me
Heart, soul and eyes
Bleeding
Drops of blood
Falling
From my canvas
Body writhing
Torture twisting my head
Looking around me
Waiting for the pool to spread
Emotions
Curling from motion, swirling around me
For all to see
If they look closely
They'll see
I'm bleeding for you
Life trickling from me

Frozen

Oh, how I long to see
The sight of you, turning to me
Turning to me with frozen lips
Your eyes ablaze against the frostbit sky
Your breath like steam
Frost tinged words forming in front of me
Tears like glass glazed over my eyes
As I read
Messages of leaving
So clearly in front of me
Suddenly my blood turns cold
In this empty state I reach out in need
But to my silent despair you pay no heed
You kiss my cheek goodbye
As if you never touched me
I watch you turn and walk away
Even though I've always known you'd leave anyway
I've felt the pain from the day we met
Until today

Sunlight illuminates my body

Sunlight illuminates my body
As I reluctantly open my eyes
To see the world around me, in its nakedness
A scream erupts inside me
The vampire's cry
And I ask myself, "Why?"
The thief bestows upon me
To steal away my peace
To wake me from my sleep
To pull up the curtain from around me
For the world, my audience, to see me
Tortured, broken and bleeding
But they cannot help me
Nor would I let them if they could

Making Love To The Wall

Spending the whole day
Walking around
With my beating heart in my chest
But it feels like grape gum on the ground

And late at night
When sadness starts to fall
My soul fills with pain
Eyes start to bleed emotions, tears and all

Lying in bed crying
Helplessly, your name I call
Drifting off to dreams of you
Within these boundaries
Wanting you to be there at dawn
Only to wake up making love to the wall

Slowly sunlight creeps in
And once again I open my eyes
Overwhelmed with disappointment, that you're not by my side
Still, waking up to something solid and strong
Once again to find my eyes
Making love to the wall

Looking

Looking
Looking for someone from which to jump beyond myself
Looking for someone to catch this drift
Looking for someone to surf the same wavelength
Looking for someone to catch my disorganized thoughts
As they spew forth
Looking
For someone
Looking to someone, to the invisible air
A person I can't see, someone to live through
After I jump beyond me
To look back and see
My tangled emotions and half empty thoughts

Bleeding heart gushes

Bleeding heart gushes
From the knife inside me
Lodged so deeply
The handle I cannot see
Hand reaches inside
Searching to find
Something to set me free
It's found
But I'm still bound
My eyes search desperately
For the clamps
To pinch off my bleeding arteries

I thought you were sweet

I thought you were sweet
Now I'm not so sure
I thought you were different
Foolishly I believed this
(They never are)
I thought you had a heart
But it was foreshadowed due to the façade
Hardened from when things were banished
'Causing you to cut people to the quick
And you wonder why you're so hypersensitive
Tripping at everything lately
I really don't think it's in your nature to be
You're just reflecting on past experiences
That haven't healed

What would you do

What would you do
If I told you
That I love you
And that I want to hold you
And show you all you have missed
Due to that heartless bitch
To hear all your dreams
And make them come true
Forever loving you
Yet I can't tell you this
For fear of being banished
For fear of you hating me

Crash And Burn

All I wanna do
Is crash and burn with you
Walk you through all the pain and hell
All the crap she hands to you
Beside you to see you through
All I wanna do
Is crash and burn with you
Working towards that common goal
As we crash into tons of obstacles
Only to see you burn in successes sweet glow
All I wanna do
Is crash and burn with you
To scorch the sheets
To call your arms home
But in cold, harsh reality
I'll be burning all alone

I never dreamed

I never dreamed
That the way your eyelashes sweep
Against your cheeks, when you read
Causing shadows
Could make me want to melt

I never dreamed
That I could meet
Someone so kind, caring, sensitive and sweet
As you
Or that when you smile at me
And your eyes crinkle and you look so cuddly
That I'd be overcome with the need
To reach out and hug you
Or when you're feeling blue
That I'd feel the need to shelter and protect you
From life's storms

And I never dreamed
That you could love me
The way I love you

But then again, I never dreamed
That this could be a reality

Stolen

My soul shrinks back
In the brightness of daylight
Oh, how I long for the darkness of night
My comfort zone
Where I can dance with my shadow
Under moonlight, in the cold
Blackness covering my troubled, tortured soul
Emotions and thoughts roam
Lurking in the shadows
Of my new home
Until the light comes
And before I know it
All is
Stolen

Shrieks of my lonely soul

Shrieks of my lonely soul
Echo on inside of me
Coldness lurks in my heart
Pain throbs throughout me
As my eyes search desperately
For someone to cling to
For someone to hold me
Longing for affection to be bestowed upon me
For a friend of the male variety
To stand beside me
From here to eternity

Once again I'm in your arms

Once again I'm in your arms
Your lips on mine
Our hearts beat in time
You start to whisper in my ear
Words of love, your soul tells you I need to hear
I'm secure in your arms, safe from all harm
Then reality hits me
Once again I'm dreaming
Of the way it could've never been

Sweet Intoxication

Why you hold me captive is a mystery to me
Your aura of kindness
Intrigues me
The warmth of your smile
Leaves me breathless
Your voice causes my heart to skip a beat
And a tightness in my chest
The smell of contradiction
Haunts my senses
Such a strong fixation
Your sweet intoxication

I'm Sorry

I'm sorry
For what I feel
I didn't mean for it to flare up this way
I'm sorry
For making you paranoid
But if you weren't you
I woudn't feel this way
I'm sorry
That I can't look away
From the heart stopping glare
You cast off
And I'm sorry
That my feelings are all in vain
But I'm even sorrier
That you'll never feel the same

Cry Myself Blind

Down my cheeks the tears flow
One by one they trickle
In time
To the chime of my sobs
That echo
On the inside dying chamber
Of me
Running, running freely
Not knowing, where they're going
In time
My eyes swell up to slits
As I cry myself blind

Just this once

Just this once
Could you do something for me?
Hold me in your arms
And satiate this need
Take me to your bed
And make love to me
Softly and sweetly
Even if you never get to know me
Even if this is a lie
Just to know that once you loved me
Might make it easier to let go
And say goodbye

Looking Pain In The Eyes

From the front
From the back
From the profile
On either side
No matter what angle
I always die
Inside or outside
I always want to cry
But to look you in the face
Is to look pain in the eyes

I took a walk in the rain

I took a walk in the rain
On this cold, raw, windy day
Trying to soothe the heartache inside
Hoping it would be torn away
And praying into my eyesight once again, you would not stray
For if you did
I might drop dead on the street
Tearlessly
For the fountain of my tears
Is raining all around me

Silent

You come into view
And push the panic button
Hush heart
Don't let him hear your tortured beating
Hush lungs
Don't let him hear your strangled breathing
Hush insides
Silently die...as if it was the last time
Stop eyes
Stop tearing
Stop lips
Hold back the words (and screams) of retaliation and hating
I silently pray
That every part of me will remain
Silent

One day you'll read this

One day you'll read this
And in the air
You'll hear a fractured heart beating, beyond repair
One day you'll read this
And out of the corner of your eye
You'll see a single teardrop, fall from the sky
One day you'll read this
And you'll see
All you once meant to me
One day you'll read this
A book of my heart's memories
One day you'll read this
As we live our happy lives separately
One day you'll read this
And you'll remember me

Nightmares

Nightmares
Of childhood past
The defiant days
When I had the guts to ask
You to the dance
Only to be turned down
The days when I denied
My intuition
And believed all his lies
The days when I had the nerve to say
"I love you"
Only to be laughed at like a clown
The days when I could dream
That two people could establish the same dream
If they didn't lose their passion-for it
The days when I believed
That I could love someone endlessly
And him me
(Only when I drifted on sparks of imagery)
If only the picture was shifted slightly

Then it became a reality-I couldn't obtain
So here I stand once again
On my last ounce of bravery
Asking the one I crave
Please, won't you love me?

Out Of The Shadows

Longing to walk the streets
To feel the wind tearing at me
As I walk silently
In my wonder, torture and pain
As towards a state of slumber
This town creeps
My presence, the shadows keep
As I walk in the night so deep
Playing hide and seek
With the moon
I know the dawn is breaking soon
As I walk aimlessly
Wishing someone would find me
Broken and bleeding
A sigh escapes
The life slipping out of me
As I crumble in the street
And lie peacefully
For soon I'll be emerging
Out of the shadows

Chameleon Soul

Sitting here
Thinking of you
Out with someone else
And it makes me want to vomit
The leftover chunks and toxins
Of my recovering heart and soul
From this poison of you
That is you
Tears start to flow
Out of frustration
'Cause I really thought I let you go
(But I guess not)
Jealously
Eats at me
Yet I have no right to be
Since I never mentioned it
And you couldn't see
Fearing
That you're going to get hurt
Being so freshly released from your personal pit of hell
Reminding myself, that I can't do a damn thing about it
(Either way)

And that my wish will never come true
So I try and get happy
Thinking
Better love will come my way
Yet no response has come my way
From the new object I'm craving
As I sit here decaying
With my chameleon soul

I woke up this morning...

I woke up this morning with a hole in my soul
So deep that a manicure and all its toxins couldn't fill it
But somehow you found your way in
To my head, heart and eyesight
And once again filled that void that is solely mine
So much so that I became nauseous and a headache in sued
As if you were a drug
Turning my brain to mush
As people screamed for their supper
So caught up in all that is you
Something I swore I would never do
Again
Then you left
My heart empty and aching
Already waiting
For the next shot of you
And wondering if I'll ever recover
Completely

There I stood

There I stood
Caught in your headlights
Panicking
Wanting to run
Or turn away
But I stood frozen
As always
In your romantic glare
Mesmerized
By those emerald tinted windows
And your sexiness
All I could do was stare
My heart beating overtime
My lungs struggling for air
Once again caught in the emotions
Never reciprocated
Never there

Squinting against the sun

Squinting against the sun
Opening my eyes
And wondering how much more of my life
Has passed me by
Feeling so low even a Prozac commercial
Can't lift me up
As I move to the shower
And start another belated day

I woke up this morning

I woke up this morning
And looked in the mirror
Just like everyday
There were tears
And a complexion
As red as can be
But as I look again I see
The imprint of the hand of fate
From when it slapped me
A cold, harsh reminder
That I'll never be your destiny

Rearview Mirror

I sit in anticipation
I sit in fear
Of the possibility of
My heart and soul and existence
Becoming a red smear
In the rearview mirror of your life
For someone else to clean up
In order to retain mine

I guess I wouldn't mind
As long as I don't have to wait too long

I Wanted To Go Together

I wanted to go together like a hand and a glove
I wanted to go together like peace and love
I wanted to go together like a sock and a shoe
I wanted to go together-my gray to your blue
The lies you've heard, to my truth
I wanted to go together like coffee and cream
My poetic lullabies to your peaceful dreams
Your soothing silence to my tortured screams
I wanted to go together like melody and lyrics
Your once constant sadness to my consistent cheeriness
I wanted to go together like ice cream to warm apple pie
I wanted to go together like a wink and a smile
I wanted to go together like a kiss and a sigh
But fate has only allowed us 'Hello' and 'Goodbye'

Remember Me

Remember me
As the sunlight opens your eyes
Remember me
As the guardian angel that walks by your side
Remember me
As a child
Whose only intention, was, in your arms, a haven, to hide
Remember me
As you watch raindrops fall from the sky
Remember me
Black as the silhouettes of trees
Remember me
The deli chick who finally got her wings
Remember me
And the strength of my smile
When I tell you goodbye
(For now)
Remember me

In every fan that cries
Remember me
Once in awhile
In the little things in life
Remember me
And how you're seen through my eyes

I just wanted to say thank you

I just wanted to say thank you
For slowly
Puking me-out of your system
Instead of –
Spitting me out
Harshly

I woke up heartsick today

I woke up heartsick today
Desolate and empty
Like a cancer coming out of remission
Or maybe LSD
I'm not sure
For the past three years it's all been the same to me
Blood frozen in my veins
My organs, fingers, toes and limbs
Chilling
So much so the 100% wool sweater couldn't keep me warm
The ache in my heart
Heavy
Pulsing constantly
Almost suffocating
Pounding out its own tortured beat
Feeling comfortably numb
Almost
The tears start to flow
As I think of how you'll never know

That I'll never be able to let you go
And how you can't see
The imprint you left on my soul
Lost in your existence
Clueless to the fact
That I'll never let you go

Desperation claws at me

Desperation claws at me
My soul desolate and empty
Dying
For some clarity
Of my meaning
To you
My heart bleeding
Amidst the confusion
And illusion
You've created
I listen to your voice
It tells me plenty
(Despite the denial and tears I cry)
(For your stupidity)
Yet I don't want to believe
It's all crashing down around me
But you've been so distant
Since the last time we met
Still stinging from your disappointment

The hugs and cuddling I can't forget
Making me think you want something more
And yet...
Wondering if I was just your teddy bear for the moment
The torture of curiosity
Of what does or doesn't stand between you and me
I wish you'd just end it

O.D.O.T.C.N.B.

Once again
Dreaming
Of
The way it
Could've
Never
Been

Love/Hate

I love you
I hate you
I love you
I hate you
I love you
I hate you
For all you do
And all you put me through
For all the lies
(And possible alibis)
The promises made
And the tattered shreds of the truth
How you loved me
And couldn't live without me
Then you cast me on the street
Like one of your lit cigarettes
Left to be burning
When I'd rather be
The smoke trapped in your lungs

Yearning
To be stuck with you forever
Leaving you never
But this could never be
For you have set me free

I Love You, But...

I love you
But
I don't deserve you
I love you
But
Your love scares me
I want to spend eternity with you
But
I don't want to end up like my parents
I love you
But
I don't want to burden you
With myself
I love you
But
You're perfect for me
But
You're my soulmate
But
You're not worth letting go
But
I'm doing it anyway

Because I love you
But
I met someone else
But
I didn't plan it
But
I still love you
But
I'm going to fade off in the fog for now

Someone's Someone Else

I'm sorry, I'm seeing someone
There's someone else
I've found someone else
She feels the same way about me as I do her
I've been in a relationship for six months
I'm flattered though
Flattered
Lovely
Always flattered
Never willing
To take the chance
On something else
If I can't be someone
Why can't I be someone's someone else?

Sitting here

Sitting here
Choking on my thoughts of you
Suffocating on my own tongue
Not sure what to say
Not sure what to do
Do I take yet another chance?
And crucify myself again?
Or so I sit back and wait
For you to make the move to at the least be friends?
Frustration clawing at me
Confusion permeates my soul
If both of us wait and not say anything
I guess we'll never know

Death runs rampant

Death runs rampant
Blistering through my veins
Eating through
Only to fizz through my pores
Revealing my feelings
My own body betraying me
Revealing
My fascination
Obsessive fixation
Of another love dying
Before it begins

More

The light in my world has gone out
Temporarily
Due to your leaving
Already I'm dreaming
Of seeing
You again
Light streaming back in
The one thing
My eyes hunger for
While my heart and soul
Long for so much more
My beautiful stranger

Heart For Rent

I didn't realize when we met
My heart was for rent
For you made a lifetime deposit
Through your kisses, eyes and promises
Then you robbed it blind
Spreading happiness anywhere you can find
Except where you found it
A building stands evicted
Overdrawn
Fro one day it was struck by lightning
For now
It's gone

Birthday Wishlist

It would make my day to see you
It would make my arms to hold you
It would make my heart for it to beat for you
It would make my lungs to breathe you
It would make my lips to kiss you
It would make my ears to hear you
It would make my senses to touch you
It would make my night to dream of you
It would make my life to keep you

You put me out

You put me out
Like the burning end of a midnight cigarette
You broke my heart
And here I am existing (trying to forget)
Praying, screaming
Pouring crimson regret and betrayal
Trying to forget
Reminding myself to breathe
For my heart is not beating inside me
As I'm wondering
Why did you leave?

Nothing Special

I forgot what it was like to feel my heart stop
And then I saw you
Again
Down the grocery aisle, talking to a friend
Of both of ours
Staring for a brief moment, then tearing my eyes away
Practically out of their sockets
'Uck' my sister said in a later phone call
He was nothing special
Still I can't shake
That old feeling
Or the thoughts of you that stick to my brain
Like spray paint graffiti in the thinnest cracks of a brick wall
Never to be washed off
'He was a dork. He was nothing special.'
My boss says in utter disgust
'No," I agree but...
Still you haunt
Still you're with me
And the tragedy is
You refer to me as
Nothing Special

You make me nauseous

You make me nauseous
You stop my heart
I still love you

You tell me you love me

You tell me you love me
And I just smile
Wishing you'd give me something other
Than all these things that will die
Sweet remarks and words of love
Dripping from your lips and landing like acid on my ears
Pretty flowers
Their petals like tears landing in death in my trash
Where one day I will be
Once you've found someone better than me
If only you would put it all on paper
Maybe I'd believe you
Maybe it would last
But even it would blow away in the crumbly cloud around me
For as always
I've found my place among the ashes

Cold

Cold
So cold
I feel like death is running through me
Solidifying the blood in my veins
Head pounding
As I'm drowning
Helplessly in the pain
Embalming me
As if I drift off to sleep
Sleep forever

Happy Ending

I'm scared
I'm jumping too soon
So many emotions pulsing through
Me
Wanting to be
So many things
And yet just wanting to be...there
Afraid I may scare you by how much I care
This soon
Ready to stand up and fight for both of you
Cry, laugh and scream with you
Always there to see you through
On this journey
To your someday 'happy ending'
Always fearing
I would never be good enough to give it to you
Like I would want to
Forever and always true
Foolishly dreaming of my own happy ending
That will never come true

Standard

Why do you hold me hostage?
To your leftover feelings
Always dumping on me
Can't you see you're burying
Suffocating
Your words like daggers
Ripping through me
Shattering to the bone
You say your feelings are neutral
But I don't know
You say it doesn't matter
We're not together
Just silence and chatter
But I feel like I'm held to such a standard
And as always I'll be left empty handed
'Cause I'll never be good enough
Even as your friend I can't compete
With the one that hasn't left
Despite your denial
And my regret

Teetering on the edge

Teetering on the edge
Standing
Looking back
Down into the pile of ashes
I'm about to be cast
Free falling
Faster Into
The lukewarm pile
Fresh black thrown upon me
Snowing from your lips
Looking down at me
Writhing in ecstasy
As always, finding my place among the ashes
To stay forever

Crash

Sick
So sick
Of being
Trapped
Locked inside
Metal, plastic, chrome and glass
Trapped in the present
Trapped in the past
Feeling everything and yet nothing at all
Longing to crash
Crash into someone
Without burning to ash
Just to feel something
Anything at all

Where I Wish It Was

Forever running in circles
Searching for what I wish was right before my eyes
My heart snagged on all that is you
In a midnight talk
A message in my 'Inbox'
Heart hemorrhaging inside me
Yet I know all is lost
For I'm not perfect
No skinny figure, no degree
Just innocence, feelings and insecurities
A thousand fires inside of me
Dreaming of the sweetest smile
A peaceful life
A morning kiss
That's where I wish it was
But am scared to dream
It will ever be

All That I'm Dying For

All that I'm living for
All that I'm dying for
Daydreams of the future
Turn into the sweetest nightmares
Brain whispering my darkest fears
Like a lullabie
Screaming like a jackhammer in the day's light
Wishing I could just pull myself apart
Silence my brain, silence my heart
Longing for your assurance and approval
To put out the smoke and fire
To silence the alarm
Longing to be wrapped in your arms
To simply be sheltered from the storm
To see your face I would be reassured
Lock the last stupid door
My ghosts are gaining

You Make Me

You make me want to
Put a scratch n sniff sticker at the bottom of a pool
And use it
You make me want to
Choke on
Food
My own saliva
Tears
Anything that will cause your lips to be on mine
Breathing into me
Just this once
No matter how much of a disappointment I may be
To you
Just to feel anything coming from you
The sweetest lie
To squelch the desire, to squelch the fire
To put out the flame
So I can die
Inside
And crawl back to the ashes
To eternally rest and hide

Acknowledgements

First, I want to thank God. For You are the reason I am able to breath and use this talent you have given me. You have blessed my life in so many ways. I love you!

To my Mom for always encouraging me. Thank you for all the notebooks, pencils, paper and ink. See, I did it! I told you I would publish one before you died.

To my wonderful husband, James, thank you for all the love and support and most of all, being proud of me.

To my in-laws, Jeff and Shirley McInerny, thank you for all that you have done for us.

To my book formatter, Maureen Cutajar (gopublished.com), thank you for making my book look awesome.

To Ravenborn at SelfPubBookCovers.com. You are so talented and your work is amazing. Thank you for making my first book look so good.

To all my family and friends. Thank you for your undying support.

To my readers, young and old. If you are going through some of the emotions that this poetry portrays, rest assured that one day you will wake up from the Lithium Dreams. And that one day there will be no more Melancholy Sunrise.

Made in the USA
Monee, IL
04 November 2020